George the Quarter
FINDS A HOME

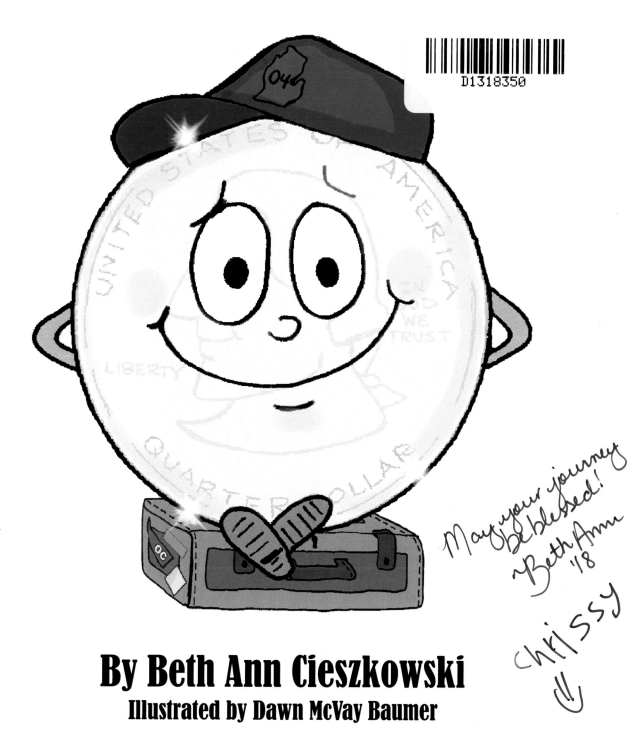

D1318350

May your journey be blessed! ~Beth Ann '18

Chrissy

By Beth Ann Cieszkowski
Illustrated by Dawn McVay Baumer

Copyright

Illustrated by Dawn McVay Baumer
ISBN 978-0-578-40086-0

Acknowledgements

To my husband, Mike Cieszkowski, thank you for the fourteen years you've listened to this story. From college rough drafts to school plays and later from illustration and design meetings to late nights revising, your patience has been steadfast and your love unconditional. Thank you for "letting" me do this.

To my parents, Larry and Lorrie Flanary, you have always supported my creative ideas and wild dreams. Thank you for seeing this one through. I will never forget telling you that 2018 was the year George was coming to life, and you said, "It's about time."

To my children, Chrissy, Grace, and Isaac, thank you for being Mommy's best audience, drawing pictures of what you saw in my words, and for your patience and love when Mommy went to meetings or spent time working on George.

To my colleague, Krista Meier, thank you for your enthusiasm and encouragement in bringing this story to life. You may never know how much that one day in the library changed my whole course.

To all of my reviewers and mentors, including Lisa Briggs, Geri Williams, Tom Shilts, Alan St. Jean, and John Fox at BookFox Editor, thank you for the constructive criticism and feedback that truly refined my work.

To Karen Bellenir, thank you for your constant support in the world of publication and book-printing.

To my friends, Cate and Kerri Waters, thank you for walking this path with me and sharing resources along the way.

To my new friend and illustrator, Dawn McVay Baumer, thank you for seeing the depth of this story, my journey, and my passion.

To all of the teachers who opened their classrooms over the past decade so that students could hear and respond to this story, thank you. It was your willingness to share your time and students that afforded me the confidence to move forward.

To my financial contributors, thank you so much for seeing the end product before its existence and trusting in me to bring it all to fruition. Your support has made this whole thing possible.

To my students- past, present, and future- who experience George, thank you for letting me be a writer who teaches, not just a teacher for whom you write.

And to my God… Thank you for orchestrating my incredibly blessed journey through this life. Thank you for the gift of words. Thank you for working all things to good in Your time. In You I trust.

For our babies who are already Home.
~B.A.C.

A busy mommy pulled me from the crowd of jumbled coins
and dropped me in the outstretched hand of her smiling little boy.
My friends called out, "Goodbye, George!" as I traveled on my way.
Each of us knew all too well there was nothing else to say.

From the checkout lane, the little boy skipped through the grocery store to the shiny, red gumball machine right beside the exit door.

His palm was rather sweaty, and he squeezed me a bit too tight.
He pushed me down into the slot and spun me out of sight.

My clinks and clanking echoed as I tumbled to the bottom.
I had seen my share of places, but this was a whole new problem.
My eyes adjusted slowly, and all around me I could see
other coins traded for gumballs stuck inside this box with me.

We greeted one another, and I practiced all their names.
In time, we became good friends and played all sorts of games.

One night we were awoken by the scratching of a key.
Two strong hands collected us despite our silent pleas.

We were all stacked inside a roll pressed together side by side.
We talked in anxious whispers as we took a mystery ride.

We stayed inside our paper bus at least a day or two-
until we heard a muffled voice ask, "How may I help you?"
A young girl's voice responded with a request so sweet and strong,
"Could I withdraw ten dollars, please; I've been waiting for so long.
I chose a puppy a week ago, and it's finally adoption day!
He's a perfect yellow Labrador. Mr. Sunshine is his name."
The teller wrapped her fingers around our tube a bit too tightly.
"We just ran out of paper tens, but this roll should suit you nicely!"

"Thank you," called the little girl dashing out the bank's front door. She hopped into her mother's car, and we ventured to the pet store.

Her excitement was infectious as she traded in our roll.
We coins had worked together to help her meet her goal.
From her hand to another's, we were knocked against a wall.
Our package ripped and we all split, but it was just a tiny fall!
Within moments we could hear robotic blips and beeps.
We had landed in a register where no one plays for keeps.

Many days and nights passed. Coins came in and some were sent.
Then a teenage girl bought dog food, and into her pocket I went.

I felt the rhythm of her walking as I explored my little space-
a ball of fuzz, a candy wrapper, and a copper penny's face! He said,

In the shadows of the pocket, we shared our stories and our tales.
Then I slipped up to the edge and saw a booth called "Ticket Sales".
Some crumpled tickets joined us and pushed me to the side.
They warned,

"You're at an amusement park. Get ready for some rides!!"

It didn't take too long before the girl was next in line.
She climbed aboard a ride that roared; she buckled just in time.
With a jolt, we sped ahead. I was thrust into the light.
I found myself upon the seat absolutely filled with fright.

The penny called from deep inside, "Be safe, my friend. Stay strong!"
And then it happened all at once- everything went wrong!
Lights were flashing all around. The coaster's music boomed.
Gravity pulled me from the ride; I knew that I was doomed.

I plummeted from the sky, afraid and all alone.
I landed- splat!- in icky mud. It chilled me to the bone.

I sank into that puddle thinking about my journey's past:
the gum machine, coin roll, and coaster. I just wanted a home to last!

I counted all the careless shoes that trampled over me that day.
Then a playful, little boy bent down with something sweet to say.
"Hello there, little quarter guy stuck down there in the mud.
I'm gonna clean you up now. Just be patient with me, Bud."

He wiped the mud from my face and shined me with his shirt.
He gently turned me over, and he brushed away the dirt.
He studied me intently. "Michigan? Two thousand four?
The place and year that I was born! I couldn't ask for anything more."

He rushed away from all the noise and showed me to his mother.
"Let's save that with your treasures; you can keep it with your others!"

They walked away and laughed about their day of rides and fun.
The boy looked down and winked at me. I knew I was the lucky one.

He tucked me in his special box with treasures all his own.
I realized then each place I'd been had helped me find my home.

ABOUT THE AUTHOR

Beth Ann (Flanary) Cieszkowski is a hard-working, God-loving, word-smithing farm girl born and raised in Hartland, Michigan. Since her childhood, she has been fascinated by the power of words and the ability to evoke emotion through writing.

She has grown up to become a spunky middle school language arts teacher. She currently resides in Okemos with her husband, Mike, doing her life's most important work raising their trio of adorable kiddos- Christina, Grace, and Isaac.

Beth Ann dreams of becoming an author when she grows up so she can spread the message of God's redeeming love in creative, metaphorical stories that touch the hearts of all ages.

Dawn McVay Baumer is a long time illustrator from Eaton Rapids, Michigan. She is the owner of "Dawn's Art To You", is also an author and travels teaching children's/adult art classes.

She is a mother of two boys and spends her free time with her family.